What If We Do
NOTHING?

ENDANGERED SPECIES

Sean Sheehan

Please visit our web site at: www.garethstevens.com.
For a free color catalog describing Gareth Stevens Publishing's list of high-quality books, call 1-800-542-2595 (USA) or 1-800-387-3178 (Canada). Gareth Stevens Publishing's fax: 1-877-542-2596

Library of Congress Cataloging-in-Publication Data

Sheehan, Sean, 1951-
Endangered species / by Sean Sheehan.
p. cm. – (What if we do nothing?)
Includes bibliographical references and index.
ISBN-10: 1-4339-0086-6 ISBN-13: 978-1-4339-0086-0 (lib. bdg.)
1. Endangered species–Juvenile literature. I. Title.
QL83.S54 2009
333.95'22–dc22 2008029167

This North American edition published in 2009 by Gareth Stevens Publishing under license from Arcturus Publishing Limited.
Gareth Stevens Publishing
A Weekly Reader® Company
1 Reader's Digest Road
Pleasantville, NY 10570-7000 USA

Produced by Arcturus Publishing Limited
26/27 Bickels Yard, 151–153 Bermondsey Street, London SE1 3HA

Gareth Stevens Managing Editor: Lisa M. Herrington
Gareth Stevens Editor: Jayne Keedle
Gareth Stevens Creative Director: Lisa Donovan

Series concept: Alex Woolf
Editor: Alex Woolf
Designer: Phipps Design
Picture researcher: Alex Woolf

Picture Credits: Corbis: 5 (Yann Arthus-Bertrand), 6 (Michael and Patricia Fogden), 8 (Gustavo Gilabert/Corbis Saba), 9 (Wolfgang Kaehler), 10 (Colin McPherson), 13 (Yvette Cardozo), 16 (DLILLC), 19 (Jeffrey L. Rotman), 21 (Stephen Frink), 22 (Ed Kashi), 26 (Ron Sachs/Corbis Sygma), 29 (EPA), 31 (Alex Hofford/EPA), 32 (Bobby Yip/Reuters), 34 (W. Perry Conway), 37 (Layne Kennedy), 39 (Momatiuk/Eastcott), 41 (Roger Tidman), 43 (Paul A Souders), 45 (Torsten Blackwood/Pool/EPA). NASA: 23 (Jeff Schmaltz, MODIS Rapid Response Team, NASA/GSFC). Shutterstock: Cover bottom left (Miranda van der Kroft), cover bottom right (Tom C. Amon), cover background (aliciahh), 15 (Christian Riedel), 25 (Simone van den Berg), 30 (Clive Gibson), 35 (Sam Chadwick), 36 (Pete Carron).

Cover pictures: Bottom left: The gorilla lives in the tropical forests and mountains of Africa. It is threatened by habitat destruction, commercial hunting, and poaching. Top right: The red-eyed tree frog is a native of lowland rain forests in Central America. Tree frogs are captured for zoos as pets, and their habitat is threatened by deforestation. Background: Leopard fur. Leopards are on the Red List of endangered species, threatened by habitat loss and hunting.

Printed in China

1 2 3 4 5 6 7 8 9 14 13 12 11 10 09 08

Contents

CHAPTER 1
Rain Forests Under Threat 4

CHAPTER 2
African Wildlife 12

CHAPTER 3
The Oceans 18

CHAPTER 4
Asia's Animals 24

CHAPTER 5
North American Wildlife 34

CHAPTER 6
Antarctica 40

Glossary 46
Further Information 46
What Would You Do? 47
Index 48

Rain Forests Under Threat

It is 2025. Despite worldwide protests, the logging of the Brazilian rain forests continues. This has caused yet another winter of floods and landslides. Rivers have become polluted and their banks have been destroyed in the flooding. The logging of so much of the Brazilian rain forest has killed a huge number of plants, including several that had proved useful in the treatment of cancer and other serious illnesses. Hundreds of species of animals and insects have also been wiped out.

In the few isolated areas of forest that remain, animals and plants are dying as their food sources and habitats are lost. Fruit-eating bats, which once played a vital role spreading seeds in the forest, have disappeared. That makes it even harder for the forest to grow back. The harlequin frog, which once provided food for predators and kept insect numbers down, is long gone. The frog's thin skin made it vulnerable to a disease-carrying fungus, which has spread due to global warming. The forest's greatest predator, the jaguar, has been hunted to extinction by farmers.

The Rain Forest

The world's rain forests are situated around the equator in South and Central America, Asia, and Africa. Rain forests have a hot, humid climate. They once covered 14 percent of the planet but now cover only 2 percent. Nevertheless, they provide a habitat (an environment offering food, shade, shelter, and protection) for half of all known species of flora and fauna (plants and animals). Because the rain forests are shrinking, many species are now under threat.

What Is an Endangered Species?

When the number of individuals in a species becomes very low and the species is at risk of dying out, the species is considered endangered. Many species have become endangered over the course

A section of the Brazilian rain forest has been cut down for its timber and to make space for crops. Similar sights can be seen in many of the world's rain forests.

of Earth's history, and many have suffered extinction (the death of a species). Over millions of years, as conditions on Earth have changed, plants and animals have either adapted or become extinct. Change has usually happened very gradually, giving time for each species to adapt.

However, some changes have been so enormous and so sudden that only a few species of plants and animals survived. One such change occurred about 65 million years ago, when the dinosaurs suddenly died out. Their extinction was probably caused by a meteor colliding with Earth or an enormous volcanic eruption that led to rapid climate change. The most recent of these sudden changes was the last Ice Age, when large numbers of big animals — such as the sabre-toothed tiger and the mammoth — became extinct. Since the ice sheets did not reach as far as the equator, many of the rain forest animals survived.

In the last few hundred years, human behavior has created a threat of mass species extinction even more sudden and destructive than the last Ice Age. No one knows how many species have become extinct. Some scientists suggest that, as each acre of rain forest is cleared, as many as 140 extinctions of tiny insects and plants could be occurring every day.

ENDANGERED SPECIES

So far, scientists concerned with extinction have examined only about 40,000 of the estimated 1.5 million species of flora and fauna that exist on Earth. The following percentages show how many of those are in danger of becoming extinct:

- 25 percent of mammals
- 12 percent of birds
- 33 percent of amphibians
- 52 percent of insects
- 51 percent of reptiles
- 33 percent of conifer trees
- 73 percent of flowering plants

Some scientists estimate that half of all living species will be extinct by 2100.

The harlequin frog, an endangered creature of the Amazon rain forest, displays its warning colors to deter predators. However, that does not offer protection against threats such as pollution, fungal disease, and trout introduced to the rivers where harlequins spawn.

Ecosystems

All of Earth's animals and plants depend on one another for their survival. Large predators, such as jaguars, need smaller animals for food. Smaller animals need plants or insects for food. Plant life depends on the large predators to keep down the numbers of grazing animals and to prevent overgrazing. In this way, groups of plants and animals live in interdependent communities called ecosystems. The needs of all the species within an ecosystem are held in a delicate balance. If one key species is lost, the whole system may be threatened. In the rain forest, bats and birds distribute seeds. The harlequin frog and other amphibians control insects. Larger predators, such as the jaguar, prey on smaller mammals that might otherwise overgraze the forest floor.

One example of species interdependence in an ecosystem involves the hyacinth macaw. This beautiful, endangered bird of the Brazilian rain forest depends on one of its predators, the toco toucan, for its home. Toucans hollow out tree trunks for their nests. The macaw uses abandoned toucan nests in the rare manduvi tree for its own nests. If the toucan or the manduvi trees became extinct, the macaw would lose its habitat. Just as the manduvi trees are dependent on other species for pollination and seed dispersal, the macaw is dependent upon the toucan and the manduvi trees for its home.

GLOBAL WARMING

Earth is getting warmer. We notice it in warmer summers, earlier springs, more violent weather, and the melting of glaciers. Part of global warming is probably natural. Earth's climate has changed many times over millions of years. We are likely now experiencing another period of change. However, most scientists agree that human activity is causing global warming to proceed at a faster pace. One reason for this is the release of greenhouse gases, which prevent heat from escaping Earth's atmosphere. One of these gases is carbon dioxide, which is released when humans and animals breathe. Carbon dioxide is also released when people burn wood, coal, oil, or natural gas.

Rain forests, along with the ocean, play an important role in taking carbon dioxide, as well as heat, out of the atmosphere. As trees make new leaves, they absorb carbon dioxide and heat energy from the Sun and lock them away for as long as the tree survives. Trees also produce oxygen – vital for humans and animals – as a waste gas. As we cut down the rain forests, their capacity to absorb heat and carbon dioxide – and to produce oxygen – is diminished.

Why the Rain Forest Is Shrinking

Honduran mahogany trees were once widespread throughout Central and South America. Today the tree is threatened with extinction because so many have been cut down to make hardwood furniture. Logging — cutting down trees for wood — is a profitable industry in the rain forest. Wood from rain forest trees is used around the world to make furniture, build houses, and make paper. Most logging is unregulated by governments. The loggers cut down everything in their path to get at the valuable wood. Their machines damage the soil, pollute rivers, and destroy habitats. Burning the unused branches sometimes causes forest fires and exposes animals to danger from the fire and from hunters. Controlled logging, where only the valuable wood is removed from the forest, is less harmful but still destructive.

Right: Banana plants are grown in a cleared area in this rain forest on the Caribbean island of Dominica. Instead of clearing the forest, the planters could have collected fruits and nuts from the rain forest to sell.

Large areas of rain forest are also cleared by agricultural companies to graze cattle or grow cash crops (crops grown for sale, not personal consumption), such as soya used for cattle feed. The environmental organization Greenpeace reports that in Brazil alone, between August and December 2007, some 2,700 square miles (7,000 square kilometers) of rain forest were cut down to provide land for cash crops. Rain forest soil is thin. After the first cash crop, large amounts of fertilizer must be added to maintain the soil's fertility. It is cheaper to cut down more forest than to import expensive fertilizer, so more forest is cut down every year.

Other threats to the rain forest come from mining and from damming rivers for electricity. Along the Amazon River, open-cast mining is a problem because land is removed to extract minerals. Stripping the soil exposes poisonous chemicals, such as sulfur. Those chemicals wash into the river, killing aquatic life. Dams destroy animal habitats. One animal threatened by both mining and damming is the pink river dolphin. The pollution destroys its prey, and the dams isolate dolphins along stretches of the river.

Below: A freshly cleared area of the Brazilian rain forest burns. Ranchers, farmers, and timber companies slash and burn large areas of the forest each year. In the background is a plantation of palms, a cash crop.

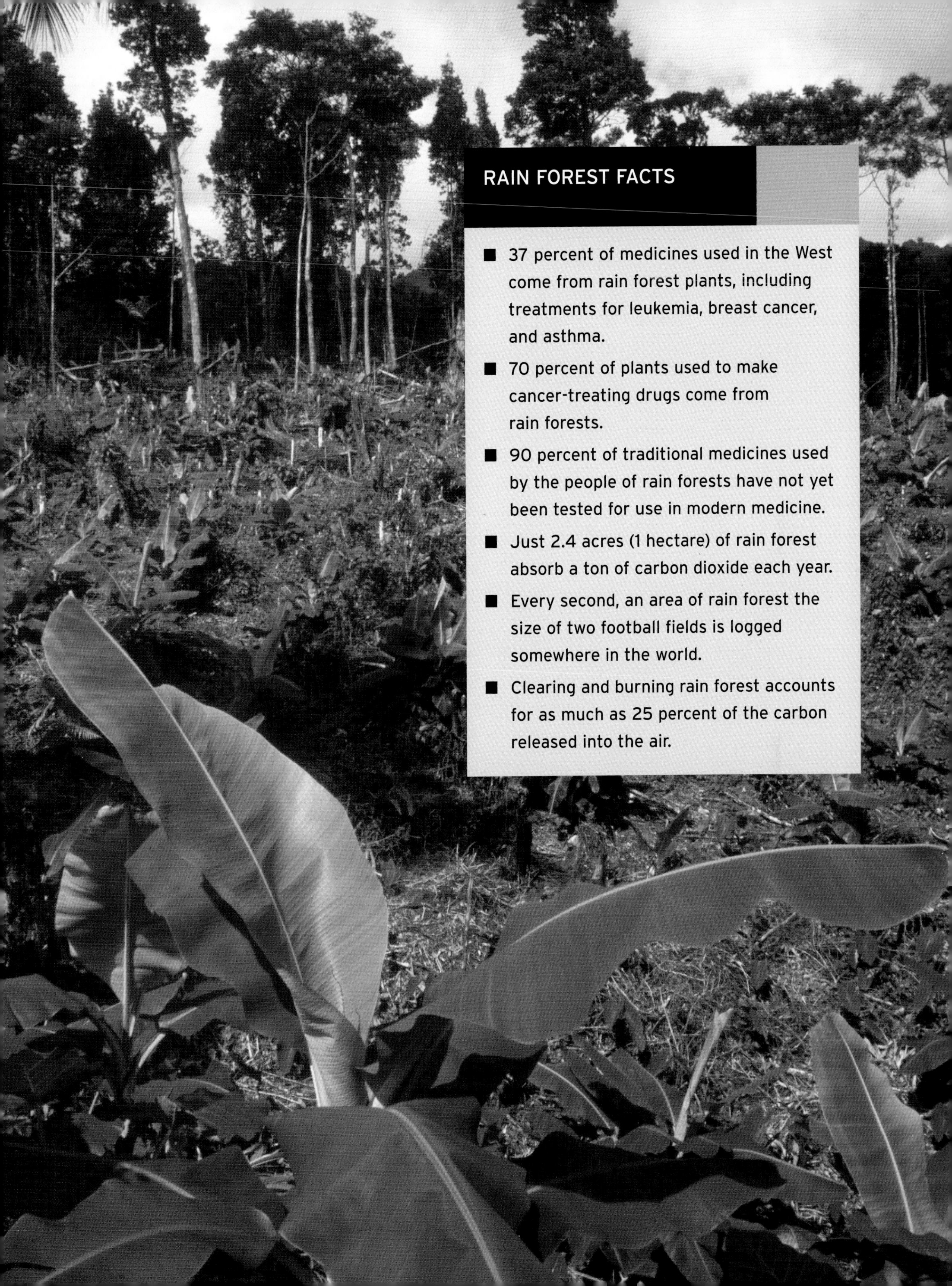

RAIN FOREST FACTS

- 37 percent of medicines used in the West come from rain forest plants, including treatments for leukemia, breast cancer, and asthma.
- 70 percent of plants used to make cancer-treating drugs come from rain forests.
- 90 percent of traditional medicines used by the people of rain forests have not yet been tested for use in modern medicine.
- Just 2.4 acres (1 hectare) of rain forest absorb a ton of carbon dioxide each year.
- Every second, an area of rain forest the size of two football fields is logged somewhere in the world.
- Clearing and burning rain forest accounts for as much as 25 percent of the carbon released into the air.

Saving the Rain Forests

It is estimated that five centuries ago, 10 million people lived in rain forests. Today, fewer than 40,000 rain forest dwellers survive. They have valuable knowledge about the forest that may soon be lost to everyone. These people have lived in the rain forest without harming it. Governments could learn from them how to protect the forests. This can only happen if the rain forest dwellers survive.

One way to prevent more rain forest destruction is to maintain the fertility of land that is already cleared. That would encourage farmers not to abandon it. This would also give them less reason to cut down trees to gain more fertile land. Some crops, such as bananas and coffee, benefit from the shade provided by older trees, so some cash-crop farming could be encouraged on the outskirts of the rain forest. Other trees, such as the Brazil nut tree, provide a valuable crop and will only survive in the deep cover of the forest.

A boy collects seeds from the annatto tree in the Amazon rain forest. The seeds are used as food coloring, dye, in cosmetics, and in medicine. People in rain forests have traditionally lived on fruits and vegetables harvested from the land.

Builders and carpenters could find alternatives to rain forest hardwoods for making houses and furniture. Governments could ban the import of hardwoods unless they are from managed forests. In those areas, the removal of valuable trees is limited, leaving enough young trees and plants for the forest to grow back. Some governments are already paying landowners not to cut down their forests.

Some experts have suggested that farming the rain forest itself — gathering its fruits and seeds and medicines — could be worth more per acre of land than logging, cash cropping, or mining.

WHAT WOULD YOU DO?

You Are in Charge

You live in a small community in South America. A logging company wants to cut down the rain forest that surrounds your village. A travel company also wants to run tours in the area for bird-watching groups interested in rare species. Both need permission from the villagers. Some people favor the logging company because they want to use the cleared land to grow bananas, oil palm trees, and soya to make money that your village desperately needs. What's your position?

- You would allow the logging company to clear cut the forest. Raising cash crops is the best way to use the land.
- You would allow the logging company to take down some trees, but only if the company agrees to use selective logging.
- You would deny the logging company permission. The tour group will provide a new source of income for the village that won't damage the rain forest.

What other ways might the villagers earn an income without harming the rain forest?

CHAPTER 2

African Wildlife

It is 2025. In Kenya, an African country that depends on tourism as a major source of its income, news reports confirm that a gang of criminals entered the largest national park armed with guns. Disguised as tourists, the gang set out to hunt the rare breeding groups of black rhinoceroses that made the park so famous. They killed the entire herd, taking their horns to sell them illegally. It is thought there are now no more black rhinos in Africa.

Africa

Africa covers 6 percent of Earth's surface and contains 14 percent of the human population. Its 46 countries include some of the poorest nations in the world. Africa is also home to some of the world's most varied wildlife. The savannahs — areas of grassland and brush — cover about 5 million square miles (13 million sq km) and support an enormous diversity of flora and fauna. About 850 African animal species are considered endangered and those are just the ones that have been discovered. The black rhino and the mountain gorilla are critically endangered animals. They are at risk of extinction in the next few years. Others, less well known to the world, such as the Marungu sunbird of Zaire, are seriously at risk from loss of habitat.

Africa also has the Sahara, the largest and oldest of the world's deserts. It is home to the endangered slender-horned gazelle, which is hunted for its horn. African coastlines provide a vast range of

THE RED LIST

The International Union for Conservation and Nature (IUCN) is an international organization that was set up in 1948. Each year it assesses the threat to endangered species by counting or estimating the number of as many species as possible. This is called the Red List. The list places animals in various degrees of endangerment, according to the numbers still surviving and the potential threats to their survival. African animals on the Red List include:

- African elephant (vulnerable)
- African wild dog (endangered)
- black-footed cat (vulnerable)
- black rhinoceros (critically endangered)
- bonobo (endangered)
- cheetah (endangered)
- lion (vulnerable)
- mountain gorilla (critically endangered)
- mountain zebra (endangered)
- pygmy hippopotamus (endangered)

habitats — from coastal lagoons and mangrove swamps to river deltas and marshland. The critically endangered Mediterranean monk seal, perhaps numbering as few as 500, inhabits the Saharan coast. The inland rain forests are the second largest in the world. Africa's highest mountain, Kilimanjaro, is home to many endangered animals, including leopards, elephants, and the rare Abbott's duiker, a type of antelope.

Ecotourism

Ecotourism has had a beneficial effect on African wildlife. Nature reserves and safari parks employ local people as rangers or as staff in the tourist lodges. Locals also sell handicrafts to visitors. The income provides a living for people who might otherwise see wildlife, such as elephants and lions, as a threat or as food. The income earned by the parks also helps pay for the cost of protecting the animals. When visitors see the different animals in the wild, they are more likely to be convinced of the need to protect them. Many of Africa's wild animals owe their survival to ecotourism.

A guest at a wildlife park in Kenya photographs a giraffe in its natural habitat. Promoters of ecotourism hope that this kind of experience will help make visitors aware of the importance of preserving the world's wild places.

Animals Versus Big Business

Africa is rich in valuable gems, minerals, and metals. This has attracted international mining companies to the continent. However, open-cast mining destroys the habitats of animals and plants. Rivers are dammed to supply water to mining camps. That causes habitat loss to some highly endangered small animals that depend on the river systems. One example is the hippo of Ghana, whose habitat will be completely flooded by the Bui Dam, which will power an aluminium-processing plant. The mining of diamonds and other minerals can expose chemicals such as sulfur. The chemicals are dumped into the waterways, harming aquatic life.

Large profits can be made from logging valuable hardwoods, such as sapelli, which is harvested from the forests of the Congo river basin in the Democratic Republic of Congo. Logging companies build roads into the forest. The roads give hunters a way to reach previously inaccessible areas. Rich individuals and companies pay high prices for ivory, rhino horn, and animal skins, even though trading those goods is illegal in many places. African governments are often torn between economic and environmental concerns. Mining and logging bring in money that their countries need. Yet government officials know those industries threaten endangered species and their habitats.

MADAGASCAR

The island of Madagascar lies off the southeast coast of Africa. It contains some of the rarest creatures in the world, many of which have only ever existed on the island. Its forests once covered almost the whole island. Today, the forests have been reduced to about 15 percent of the land area, and 11 species of animals are on the IUCN Red List. Loss of habitat caused by forest and bamboo clearance for farmland poses the greatest threat to vulnerable animals. The government of Madagascar, responding to the danger of species extinction, has begun creating wildlife reserves. The government hopes the reservation will create income and employment for the people of Madagascar and will help protect the island's animals.

Animal Versus Human Needs

The growing human population poses another threat to the animals of the African wilderness. Some experts estimate that Africa's population may double by 2050. Cities, towns, and villages are expanding. The need for farmland grows in proportion to the population. Throughout sub-Saharan Africa, grassland is being lost to agriculture. Bushland and forests are being cut down for firewood and to clear fresh land for farming.

As humans and wildlife move closer together, animals such as elephants and larger predators can pose a threat to farmers, their homes, and crops. Sometimes animals are hunted by villagers seeking safety for their families. As the human population increases, people are also killing more wild animals, such as apes and zebras, for food.

THE GREATER BAMBOO LEMUR

The greater bamboo lemur is one of the most endangered animals in the world. This monkey-like creature's only food source is the giant bamboo, a plant that is being cut down at a rapid rate to make way for farmland. The lemur lives in one area of southern Madagascar and its numbers are estimated at about 1,000. It is one of the rarest animals in the world.

The ring-tailed lemur, although not as threatened as the greater bamboo lemur, is also in danger of extinction. The ring-tailed lemur inhabits forested areas in southwest Madagascar, many of which have been cleared.

Pygmy Hippopotamus

Many of Africa's large mammals are threatened by habitat loss and poaching (illegal hunting). The pygmy hippo lives in West Africa, but only in the forested river areas of Liberia and around the Niger river delta. The IUCN estimates that only 2,000 to 3,000 remain in the wild. The pygmy hippo is threatened by a number of developments. Liberia's rain forest has been heavily logged, leaving fewer areas in which the hippo can survive. The nation was also at war almost continuously from 1989 to 2003. That disrupted food supplies for many people, and the pygmy hippo was hunted for its meat.

THE MEDICINAL VALUE OF BLACK RHINO HORN

Black rhino horn is highly valued in traditional Chinese medicine. Experiments by scientists show that very large quantities of the horn can reduce fever. An aspirin, however, works just as well – and no rhinos are killed to make aspirin.

The black rhino was once a thriving species throughout central and eastern Africa. However, the high value of its horn has made it a target for illegal hunting and left it vulnerable to extinction.

Black Rhinoceros

The black rhinoceros, unlike the pygmy hippo, can survive in a variety of habitats, including semi-desert, savannah, and forests. Yet its numbers have also fallen drastically. There are now as few as 3,700 rhinos, and they live almost entirely within game reserves. The danger to the black rhino is from poachers. They illegally sell its horn for large sums (see box, page 16).

In 1973, the Convention on International Trade in Endangered Species (CITES) was signed by 63 countries. The countries agreed, among other things, to ban trade in all rhino products. Unfortunately, the ban has increased the price of rhino horn on the black (illegal) market, driving poachers to ever-greater efforts to obtain the horns. Some African countries, such as Namibia and Zimbabwe, have removed their rhinos' horns so that the poachers will leave them alone. Other countries carry out a shoot-to-kill policy on poachers. Zoos around the world have made efforts to preserve the black rhino through captive breeding programs. The United States has imposed trade sanctions against countries such as Taiwan, where the trade in rhino products, while illegal, is still widespread.

WHAT WOULD YOU DO?

You Are in Charge

The government of an African country is considering letting a mining company build a dam on one of its major rivers. The dam will flood hundreds of square miles of a national park, including areas that are known to be the only habitat of a rare plant. You are a member of a local environmental group. Members have made the following points in their argument against the dam project. How can your group increase the public's awareness about the environmental risks surrounding the dam?

- Workers in the national park will lose their jobs and homes. The national park brings in most of its income from tourism.
- Where the dam floods forested areas, the water will become polluted with rotting debris and important habitats will be lost forever.
- Water supplies to a neighboring country will be affected.

CHAPTER 3

The Oceans

It is 2025. The International Union for Conservation of Nature (IUCN) has added herring, tuna, and salmon to its list of critically endangered species. Cod is now extinct. Fishing fleets around the world lie idle as fishing is no longer profitable. Coastal villages are abandoned. Their inhabitants headed to cities in search of work and food. Japan, Norway, and Russia send out whaling fleets in an effort to use whale meat as a replacement for fish.

Endangered Oceans

The ocean is as endangered as the creatures that live in it. It is a complex ecosystem containing many interdependent species. Fish, shellfish, seabirds, whales, turtles, seaweed, algae, plankton, and coral reefs all depend on each other for survival. Marine life has been extensively researched since 2005 for inclusion in the IUCN Red List of endangered species. In 2007, several kinds of coral and several sharks and rays were added to the endangered list.

Several kinds of algae were also added to the list. This is an even greater concern for the world. Algae are the lungs of the ocean in the same way that the rain forests are the lungs of the land. Algae take in carbon dioxide and sunlight to reproduce and release oxygen into the atmosphere. They are at the bottom of the ocean's food chain. If algae become endangered, then all the creatures in the food chain are threatened, too. Algae and the other inhabitants of the ocean are threatened by pollution, overfishing, global warming, oil exploration, and tourism.

The Price of Fish

Overfishing is currently the biggest threat to marine life. Technological advances and greater demand for fish from an increasing world population has brought some fish to near-extinction in certain areas. This, for example, is the

SOME OCEAN FACTS

- Oceans cover 75 percent of the planet.
- Fish and shellfish provide about 16 percent of the world's protein needs.
- Ocean algae may produce as much as 90 percent of the atmosphere's oxygen.
- The ocean absorbs incalculable amounts of carbon dioxide from the atmosphere.
- Oceans have the potential to provide as-yet-unknown medical products.
- The ocean helps regulate our climate by taking in heat from the Sun and releasing it slowly.

case with the Atlantic sturgeon around the coasts of Canada. Since the early 1900s, many countries have established fishing quotas — restrictions on the number of fish that can be caught by fishing fleets. Some have introduced regulations limiting the size of nets to give younger and smaller fish the opportunity to escape being caught.

In 2007, an international agreement banned bottom trawling, a highly destructive form of fishing, in the South Pacific. An estimated 27 million tons (24.5 million tonnes) of sea creatures are killed by trawlers each year by becoming accidentally caught in the nets. Those include sharks, rays, dolphins, turtles, and seabirds.

In Massachusetts Bay, cod fishermen clean their catch. In 2000, the World Wildlife Fund (WWF) placed cod on its endangered list, stating that the global cod catch had fallen by 70 percent since 1970. The WWF claimed that if this trend continued, cod stocks would disappear by 2019.

Whales

Whales are hunted largely for their meat. Like other forms of fishing, whale hunting has become more efficient, with bigger ships, stronger harpoons, and better detection equipment. Smaller whales get caught in fishing nets, and others are killed by collisions with ships. Five species of whale are considered endangered, and many others are at risk. In 1986, nearly 80 countries banned whaling. Since that time, scientists believe that whale numbers have increased. The countries that traditionally hunted whales, such as Greenland, Iceland, Japan, and Norway, want the ban lifted. A 2006 report commissioned by the Convention on Migratory Species concluded that whale-watching trips for tourists can bring in much higher profits than whale hunting.

Polar Bears

Polar bears, the world's largest land carnivores, live on the Arctic sea ice. Polar bears number more than 20,000, enough to keep them off the endangered section of the IUCN Red List. Nevertheless, they are a threatened species. Polar bears hunt in autumn, winter, and spring. They catch seals, fish, and other marine creatures. In summer, when the ice fields melt, polar bears return to the landmass of the Arctic and live off their body fat.

Each year, however, due to global warming, the ice recedes by about 3 percent. That shrinks the polar bears' hunting grounds. The higher temperatures melt their dens, exposing their young to the weather and predators. Scientists estimate that the polar bears' habitat will be gone in 100 years. Since 1972, the United States has banned the hunting of polar bears. Russia allows limited hunting by indigenous (native) groups. Canada and Greenland, the other countries with polar bear populations, allow polar bear hunting for sport.

THE DUGONG

The dugong is a marine mammal similar to a manatee. It lives in the shallow waters around the coral reefs of Australia, East Africa, and the islands of Indonesia. It has been hunted for centuries for its meat, skin, bones, and oil. Many of its habitats are now protected. The total population of dugongs is thought to be about 160,000. Nevertheless, the dugong's survival is still threatened by hunting, habitat destruction, entanglement in nets, and collisions with boats.

Coral

Coral are tiny animals related to sea anemones and jellyfish. Corals cover about 100,387 square miles (260,000 sq km) of the ocean floor in shallow, nutrient-poor seas around the equator. Experts estimate

that about 500,000 marine species live among the coral reefs. People are threatening coral reefs in various ways. Some hunt reef fish with chemicals that destroy the corals. Coral reefs often become polluted by tourists who populate coastal resorts. Global warming is also causing problems for coral reefs, raising water temperatures and increasing acid levels. Carbon dioxide from the air dissolves in sea water to form an acid called carbonic acid. Carbon dioxide released by the burning of fossil fuels causes the sea to become increasingly acidic. The acid eats into the coral and into the millions of shellfish that live among the coral. About 10 percent of the world's coral reefs are already dead and another 60 percent are endangered. Many countries with coral reefs in their waters have created marine parks to help protect them.

The bleached staghorn coral is a victim of global warming. Higher sea temperatures have killed the algae that live in the coral. The coral depends on algae for its survival.

A Toxic Soup

Until 2006, when international controls came into effect, millions of tons of waste were dumped into the ocean each year. That included by-products of oil refineries, nuclear waste, agricultural waste, and sewage. All this pollution has taken its toll on fish numbers and has led to high levels of toxic chemicals in large fish.

When algae encounters sewage, the nutrients in the sewage cause the algae to multiply far beyond normal levels. This causes algae blooms (a rapid growth of algae) to develop on the surface of the sea. Too much

Pollution from this gas and oil plant in Nigeria has caused fish numbers in the area to shrink. The village beside the plant depends on fish, such as the bonga for food and income. While these fish are not yet threatened with extinction, the local community, which depends on clean waters and a good catch, is suffering.

FOOD CHAINS

The smallest creatures in the sea are known as phytoplankton. Those are tiny plants that use sunlight, nutrients from the ocean, and carbon dioxide to reproduce. Phytoplankton are eaten by tiny marine animals called zooplankton. Those get eaten in turn by bigger creatures such as fish. Small fish are eaten by larger fish or other marine creatures such as turtles or whales. In polluted seas, each creature in the food chain will absorb pollutants during the course of its life. The animals at the top of the chain, such as whales, tuna, and sharks, have the highest levels of pollutants in their systems, because everything they have eaten has also absorbed pollutants. This may affect their growth and reproduction and may ultimately kill them.

WHAT WOULD YOU DO?

You Are in Charge

You are a member of a group that regulates whaling. Several groups have asked you to allow them to hunt whales that have recently been removed from the endangered species list. Although the whales have increased in number, their populations remain low. Which groups, if any, are you most likely to permit to hunt whales again?

- Small groups of Inuits who depend on whales for food, heating, clothing, and income.
- Commercial whalers who use modern fishing techniques.
- Countries such as Norway, which claim that whaling is a vital part of their culture.

What arguments might you expect to hear from environmental groups and whale watching businesses about a proposal to allow more hunting? What's your opinion?

algae deprives other marine life of oxygen and creates dead areas. In 2006, nearly 200 dead zones were observed in an aerial survey. One of the dead zones was more than 69,500 square miles (180,000 sq km) in size. Fortunately, most dead zones are temporary. The excess nutrients are eventually consumed or dispersed. Since 1975, international regulations have restricted the amount and type of waste material that can be released into the sea. By 2001, 78 countries had agreed to abide by these rules to help prevent algae blooms.

This algae bloom (seen here as a light blue area) off the coast of France and Britain was so big that a satellite was able to photograph it. The bloom was probably caused by sewage or chemical fertilizers leaking into the sea.

CHAPTER 4

Asia's Animals

It is 2025. Orangutans have become extinct in the wild. They lost their habitat with the destruction of the Southeast Asian rain forest and were hunted for sale in the exotic pet trade. The last survivors, numbering only 18, have been brought together at the Sepilok orangutan sanctuary in Sabah, Borneo. Conservationists hope that successful breeding at Sepilok will increase the number of orangutans. Scientists also plan to begin experimenting with cloning to further boost the orangutan population. Visitors to the Sepilok sanctuary will need to book years in advance and pay high entrance fees to see the orangutans.

Gentle Giants of the Rain Forest

Orangutans once inhabited forested areas in China, Thailand, Malaysia, Borneo, and Indonesia. Gentle, funny, sociable creatures, the orangutan is the largest tree-dwelling animal in the world and the only great ape to live outside Africa. Today, fewer than 60,000 orangutans exist in just two places: Borneo and the Indonesian island of Sumatra. Because their habitat is increasingly threatened by logging, they are expected to become extinct in the wild by about 2025. Female orangutans produce, on average, only one infant every seven years. The young stay with their mother, learning how to survive, until at least age 10. In addition to the danger posed by logging, orangutans are under threat from the illegal pet trade.

SEPILOK ORANGUTAN REHABILITATION CENTRE

Loggers often kill adult orangutans and take the babies to sell as pets – a practice that is illegal. Some of these orphaned orangutans are rescued and taken to the Sepilok Orangutan Rehabilitation Centre. Based in a tiny reserve of 16.6 square miles (43 sq km) in the north of Borneo, Sepilok shelters the orphans until they learn to fend for themselves. The tame, helpless animals are gradually taken deeper into the forest as they learn to find food, build nests, and avoid human contact. Borneo is one of only two places in the world where orangutans can be seen in their natural habitat.

An orangutan mother has her hands full with two babies to rear. If they are female, they will stay with her for a decade or more. Sons will go off to find mates at about age 10. A female orangutan will have only about four or five babies in her lifetime.

EXOTIC PETS

Annual figures for animals captured and sold as pets each year are as follows:

- 4 million birds
- 640,000 reptiles
- 40,000 primates
- 350 million tropical fish

The annual profits for the exotic pet trade are about $6 billion. Most reptiles die within a year of capture, and other pets are abandoned or suffer in captivity. Many species carry diseases that can be transmitted to humans or livestock.

These pandas were born in the China Research and Conservation Center for the Giant Panda in Wolong, China. They currently live at the National Zoo in Washington, D.C. They have produced one cub during their stay at the zoo.

Asia and Its Wildlife

Asia is the world's largest and most densely populated continent. It contains more than 60 percent of the world's population and nearly 30 percent of Earth's total land area. India and China, the world's two most populous countries, are undergoing huge economic growth. This has led to an expansion of their towns and cities. Wilderness areas have been developed for agriculture or settlement, threatening wildlife habitats. As a result, both countries are home to some critically endangered species, including the tiger, the giant panda, and the Asian elephant.

Most of the world's illegal trade in endangered animals takes place in Asia. Many of these animals, such as tigers and rhinos, are highly prized in traditional forms of medicine.

Giant Pandas

One of the most well-known of all endangered species is the giant panda. Conservationists estimate that between 2,000 and 3,000 remain in the wild. Pandas are protected under the Convention on International Trade in Endangered Species (CITES) agreement (see box) and are on the IUCN Red List. The panda's chief source of food is bamboo. It is very poor in nutrients, and pandas must eat up to 84 pounds (38 kilograms) of bamboo every day. About once a decade, the bamboo plant suddenly produces flowers then dies away, depriving pandas of food. Unless they find an alternative source of bamboo, many pandas starve. Pandas, like orangutans, breed slowly, so their numbers are not easily restored after such a loss.

For many years, China attempted to protect giant pandas by bringing as many as possible into captivity. The government has created 40 reserves for pandas, removing human residents from those areas. Zoos in other countries can hire pandas for a period of 10 years at a cost of $1 million or more per year. The zoos must agree to return to China any baby pandas born during that time once they are three years old. The United States has passed a law that prevents zoos from hiring pandas unless most of the fee goes to panda conservation in China.

Placing pandas in captivity has not completely solved the problem. Pandas in zoos and reserves have generally failed to reproduce. Also, many of the panda cubs that were born in captivity died, probably because of the mother's inexperience or poor handling by zookeepers. Chinese conservationists have been researching ways to improve panda cub survival rates. Their efforts appear to be successful. A 2006 survey suggests the numbers of giant pandas, both in the wild and in captivity, are increasing.

CITES

Since 1973, an international agreement has been in place to regulate trade in endangered species. The Convention on International Trade in Endangered Species of Wild Fauna and Flora (CITES) sets certain rules for member states to follow. CITES has banned or controlled trade of 5,000 animal species and 28,000 species of plants and their products. The treaty has been signed by 172 countries and has probably saved many wild creatures from extinction. CITES makes a positive contribution to the preservation of wildlife by banning countries from trading certain species.

Asian Elephants

Tamed and trained Asian elephants are fairly common in India, Sri Lanka, Vietnam, Thailand, Burma, Malaysia, and Nepal. In the wild, though, they are endangered. Unlike the larger African elephant, which is hunted for its ivory tusks, Asian elephants are mostly threatened by habitat loss. Only some of the male Asian elephants have tusks and no females have them, so hunting is less profitable. Elephants are migratory animals. Moving continually from one food and water source to another often brings them into close contact with people. Asian elephants often clash with humans at roadsides, on railway tracks, or while grazing in fields of grain. In India, an estimated 200 elephants and 300 humans die each year as a result of encounters between the two. Currently, only about 48,000 Asian elephants remain in the wild. Another 15,000 live in game reserves or work in logging operations.

INBREEDING

Inbreeding is breeding that occurs between closely-related animals. Animals inbreed when the numbers of a particular species become very low, or they live in isolated groups. Inbreeding is common in many captive breeding programs. In some cases, animals have been traded between one zoo and another for generation after generation. Inbreeding can lead to physical defects in offspring, such as weak bones and blindness. Many offspring die young. Using DNA testing, scientists in charge of captive breeding programs are now better able to ensure that isolated animals breed with unrelated mates. The result is stronger, healthier offspring that are more likely to survive in the wild.

Rewilding the Tiger

Tigers were once widespread across Asia. Now they live in small numbers in wildlife reserves where they are protected from hunters. Tigers are hunted for their skins, and for their meat and bones, used in traditional medicine. Estimates of their numbers in the wild range from 2,500 to 5,000. Four subspecies of tiger are already extinct.

India has 25 wildlife parks, where human settlement is not allowed. The Indian government's Project Tiger was introduced in the 1970s. The organization claims that the Bengal tiger population in those parks increased steadily until 2007. Numbers began to fall in 2008.

In China, efforts are being made to place some of the tiny numbers of South China tigers back into the wild. The South China tigers held in zoos and tiger breeding farms are being sent to special game reserves in Africa. Conservationists hope that the cubs of these tigers will develop as completely wild animals before being returned to China. Experts predict that unless this project proves successful, the South China tiger will become extinct in the near future.

Cathay, a 10-month-old South China tiger, learns to hunt for herself so that she can be returned to the wild. She is one of only about 90 still surviving in the world.

Proboscis Monkeys

Proboscis monkeys are a curious-looking species with large overhanging noses, webbed feet, and big pot bellies. They live in forested areas along coastlines and rivers, chiefly on the island of Borneo. Proboscis monkeys have been hunted for food and are easy targets because of their lack of shyness and their tendency to travel in groups.

Like orangutans, they suffer from the destruction of their habitat as towns expand and new oil palm plantations are established. In just one region of Borneo, the state of Sabah, 16 percent of the total land area is taken up by oil palm plantations. Sixty percent of these plantations are on land that was once forest and home to proboscis monkeys.

New laws in Sabah protect the species and conservation groups have established several game reserves in its preferred habitat. Ecotourism offers hope for the survival of the proboscis monkey, as long as it is managed well. About 7,000 proboscis monkeys still exist in the wild. They are on the IUCN Red List.

A proboscis monkey climbs a tree in a forest in Borneo. In Sarawak, northeast Borneo, the monkeys are victims of habitat loss and hunting. The proboscis monkey population has declined from 6,500 in 1977 to about 1,000 in 2006.

River Dolphins

Two of the world's three species of river dolphin once lived in Asia. The Yangtze River dolphin, also known as the baiji, used to inhabit about 1,056 miles (1,700 km) of the Yangtze River in China. Traditionally the river dolphins were treasured. Beginning in the 1950s, however, people were encouraged to hunt them. Since the 1980s, the land along the Yangtze has grown increasingly industrialized and become very polluted. Water levels have dropped due to climate change and heavy silt deposits. Both the baiji and the fish it fed on have suffered as a result. The baiji also often collided with heavy river traffic and became trapped in fishing nets, accelerating its decline. By 1997, a survey of the river found only 13 animals. In 2007 conservationists declared the baiji "functionally extinct," meaning that the population (if any still existed) was no longer able to sustain itself.

The baiji, or Yangtze River dolphin, survived on Earth for about 20 million years. A 2007 survey could find no surviving dolphins.

In India, the Ganges River dolphin is doing slightly better. Current estimates suggest there may be as many as 2,000 surviving in the wild. However, their numbers have also declined due to discharges from factories into the Ganges, dams built across India's rivers, the silting up of river beds, and illegal hunting.

THE SLENDER LORIS

In the forests of Sri Lanka, only dwindling numbers of the slender loris survive. Locals regard this tiny monkey-like creature as a sign of bad luck. It is usually killed on sight. The slender loris's parts are used in traditional medicine. Its eyes are considered to possess special healing qualities. Its flesh is thought to be a cure for asthma. However, like so many other highly endangered species, the greatest threat to the survival of the slender loris is habitat loss.

The Price of a Fur Coat

The most remote areas of Asia, where animals ought to be safest from human hunters, are the mountainous regions. However, the profits to be made from the body parts of some of the rarer creatures of Asia's mountains tempt many hunters. Snow leopards, which live in the high mountains of Central and South Asia, are hunted for their valuable furs and body parts. A snow leopard fur coat sold in a retail store can cost as much as $50,000. Snow leopards live in the mountains above the tree line at heights of about 8,850 feet (2,700 meters) above sea level. Between 3,500 and 5,000 remain alive in the wild. Their numbers are falling due to illegal hunting of both the leopards and their prey. Experts believe that the snow leopard population is still large enough for the species to survive, as long as demand for its fur does not increase.

These protesters in Causeway Bay, one of Hong Kong's popular shopping areas, cram themselves into a cage to call attention to the poor treatment of animals in the fur trade.

Learning to Live With Nature

Like the highly endangered plants and animals of other continents and ecosystems, Asian species are threatened by human activity. Population growth and economic expansion have often led to the pollution of wildlife habitats. Habitats have also been lost to development and agriculture.

There were few protests when the people of North America and Europe cut down large areas of forest in the 1800s. At the time, few people cared about or understood the damage this would do to the species that lived there. People in Asia want to live the same comfortable lives that people in Europe and North America enjoy. Population growth and economic expansion will continue, with damaging consequences for wildlife.

There is hope for the future, however. People are beginning to realize that their desire for economic prosperity and the needs of wildlife don't have to conflict. Efforts are being made to encourage responsibly managed ecotourism. That gives local people a way to make money by conserving regional wildlife. Places such as the Bukit Saban Resort in Sarawak, Malaysia, bring tourists interested in wildlife into the forest. Local people lead the hikes, entertain the visitors, and sell handicrafts.

WHAT WOULD YOU DO?

You Are in Charge

Many poor people in Thailand, India, and Malaysia live on the borders of forested land, close to the natural habitat of the highly endangered Asian elephant. The settlements break up the elephants' migratory routes, and villagers take the elephants' food sources for firewood. Hungry elephants sometimes attack the villagers' crops and homes. Villagers respond by hunting the elephants. What measures do you think a concerned government might take to help both the villagers and the elephants coexist?

- Move people away from animal migratory pathways so elephants are farther from human habitation.
- Offer the villagers compensation and relocation to safer areas with sustainable water and wood supplies.
- Build ecotourist lodges in the area to bring in revenue for the threatened villagers.
- Relocate the elephants to enclosed nature reserves.

What other suggestions could you make to the government?

CHAPTER 5

North American Wildlife

It is 2025. Scientists have surveyed the environmental impact of the 30 oil fields established in the Arctic National Wildlife Refuge in Alaska in 2010. The survey revealed that toxic substances have harmed the environment. Acids, lead, pesticides, solvents, and diesel fuel have leaked into the soil from the vehicles and settlements associated with the oil fields. According to wildlife surveys, the endangered musk ox that once inhabited Alaska has disappeared. Many of the 135 species of birds that migrate through the area, or use it as a nesting site, have declined sharply. Indigenous people have also abandoned their traditional lifestyles. They now find work chiefly in the oil fields. Two of the fields have stopped producing oil after only 15 years. The operation of several others may soon end.

Alaska

The Arctic National Wildlife Refuge covers nearly 30,900 square miles (80,000 sq km) inside the Arctic Circle. It includes six different ecological zones, from coasts and marshlands through upland hills and tundra, to vast forests. The refuge sits to the east of the Prudhoe Bay oil fields, the largest oil deposits in the United States.

Short-tailed albatrosses look for food in the Arctic National Wildlife Refuge in Alaska. They migrate here from their breeding grounds on the tiny Japanese island of Torishima. There are less than 2,000 short-tailed albatrosses remaining on Earth. The species' survival would be threatened by any damage to the refuge.

The Trans-Alaska Pipeline carries oil from Prudhoe Bay to the port of Valdez. From there, the oil is shipped to refineries around the United States. Since it opened in 1977, the pipeline and oil tankers have spilled or leaked more than a million barrels of oil into the environment.

Controversy rages over whether Alaska's oil resources should be exploited. The issues for the United States are similar to those faced by other countries. A vast, unspoiled piece of land offers short-term profits and economic benefits to the country. But this would come at a great cost to the area's wildlife. The International Union for Conservation and Nature (IUCN) has registered more than a dozen species of wildlife in the refuge on its Red List. Those animals include the short-tailed albatross, Steller's sea lion, six species of whale, and the leatherback turtle. The IUCN is considering adding additional species to the list.

UNITED STATES OIL CONSUMPTION

The United States consumes about 20 million barrels of oil a day, or about 25 percent of the world's total output. Five million barrels come from domestic oil wells in Alaska and other U.S. states. The oil reserves in the Arctic Wildlife Refuge are estimated at between 4 and 11 billion barrels. That is enough to provide 5 percent of America's oil for roughly 12 to 30 years. Put another way, Alaska's oil reserves would supply U.S. oil demands for about 525 days at most. Many conservationists argue that it is not worth damaging the Arctic Wildlife Refuge for so little oil.

Bison graze at Yellowstone National Park. In winter, the park can support only about 3,000 animals. Each year, some of the herd are killed as they wander out of the park and into nearby grazing land.

The American Bison

Bison, or buffalo as many people call them, are large, grazing mammals that were once a vital food source for Native Americans. Tens of millions of bison roamed as far north as Canada and as far south as Mexico. In the 1800s, they were hunted almost to extinction. By the 1890s only tiny herds of bison survived. Their numbers began to increase at the turn of the 20th century as a result of captive breeding programs. Today bison are no longer critically endangered, but many of them have interbred with domestic cattle. Very few pure species of bison remain. The bison in Yellowstone National Park are, in fact, the only surviving pure-bred herd.

As the numbers of the hybrid animals expand outside of wildlife parks, they have begun competing with domestic livestock for grazing and water. Bison can carry the cattle disease brucellosis, which can infect domestic herds. Also, bison occasionally kill humans when they feel threatened. For those reasons, many farmers have recently called for action to cull bison herds. Some states have even started to permit bison hunting on a limited scale.

Wolves

Like many other animals that were regarded as a threat to the human population, some species of wolf were wiped out in the United States by the 1950s. Packs of eastern timber wolves, however, survive in Ontario and Quebec in Canada. There have been some sightings of these animals in the northern United States. Ecologists are studying the possibility of reintroducing them to wilderness areas in the Northeast.

In the southeastern United States, the red wolf survives in very small numbers. A few have been reintroduced into the wild from zoos. A small population established in the Great Smoky Mountains in the 1990s failed to survive. It is important that the wolves are resettled in wilderness areas, far from human settlements. They hunt their prey in packs and can pose a threat to livestock and humans.

By 1980, the red wolf had been completely wiped out in its natural homelands in the southeastern United States. Captured animals, bred in captivity, have been released back into the wild. However, the red wolf remains critically endangered, with as few as 250 animals left, most in captivity.

LIVING WITH WILDLIFE

Many state governments have taken steps to protect their wildlife. They have produced rules for people whose homes are alongside remote areas. Here are some survival rules issued by the state of California for people who live near mountain lions:

- Don't feed deer. It is illegal in California because it will attract mountain lions.
- Make gardens deer-proof by avoiding plants that deer like to eat.
- Keep bushes trimmed to reduce hiding places for mountain lions.
- Don't leave small children or pets outside unattended.
- Provide sturdy fences and covered shelters for livestock.
- Don't allow pets outside between dusk and dawn.
- Feed pets inside the house to avoid attracting small animals, which are potential prey for mountain lions.

Foreign Invaders

Some animal species are threatened not by the loss of a key species that they depend on, but by the arrival of one. An example of this in the United States can be found in the salt marshes of Chesapeake Bay. There, a large rat-like creature called the nutria, once native only to South America, has colonized several salt marshes. The nutria eats marsh plants whose roots form the stable base of the marshlands. As a result, the nutria invaders have caused the erosion of some 7,000 acres (283 hectarces) of breeding and feeding grounds for fish, crabs, and wetland birds, including the endangered black rail. The North American nutria population has expanded enormously. In the salt marshes alone, they number in the tens of millions. Ecologists estimate that the annual cost of controlling the nutria and other invasive species, and attempting to repair the damage they cause, comes to about $138 billion.

TOUGH LOVE

The United States has hundreds of wildlife reserves. Many of these protected areas are open to the public. Visitors to these places often pose the primary danger to the wildlife within them. Walkers erode pathways, causing damage to delicate plants. Garbage left by visitors upsets the food chain. Recreational vehicles, such as all-terrain vehicles and dirt bikes, hit animals, crush plants, and pollute the air. Boating enthusiasts introduce foreign shellfish attached to the hulls of their boats. Not all the damage is done by visitors, however. Special sprays aimed at stopping brush fires pollute the land and kill native species. That can allow invasive foreign plants to gain a foothold in the environment.

The California Condor

The California condor is a large and critically endangered bird of prey that lives near the Grand Canyon and the coastal mountains of California. Condors often feed on carrion (dead animals) that have been shot by humans. The lead pellets in the carrion poison the condors. Also, many condors collide with power lines. Another threat to condor survival is egg stealing by humans. By 1989, there were just 25 of these birds left. Conservationists decided to capture them and place them in breeding programs in zoos. Since 1991, carefully monitored groups of condor have been released back into the wild and are now successfully breeding on their own. Experts now believe the number of California condors has risen to more than 300.

This tagged California condor was born in captivity and released into the wild in the Grand Canyon in Arizona. Condors mate for life, and the female lays only one egg every two years. It took many years, and careful supervision, for the species to recover following its near extinction.

WHAT WOULD YOU DO?

You Are in Charge

You are on the governing body of a large national park. Visitors have unknowingly damaged the park's environment. They have worn down pathways, causing erosion during rainfall. Their vehicles have hit animals, and their noise has frightened birds. Some individuals have been injured by animal attacks. How would you solve those problems? Think about the pros and cons of the following solutions. What other compromises could you consider?

- Increase the entrance fees to the park to raise money to repair the damage.
- Limit road access to areas where animals are least likely to be disturbed.
- Ban all vehicles from the park and limit where people can walk on trails.
- Close the park to visitors.

Should national parks be used by people for recreation, or should their purpose be to only preserve and protect the land as a habitat for plants and animals? What is your opinion?

CHAPTER 6

Antarctica

It is 2025. Krill, a tiny shrimp-like creature and a vital part of the Antarctic food chain, has been declared endangered. Whales, several species of seal, squid, penguins, albatrosses, and other birds – all of which depend on krill – have declined nearly to the point of extinction. The ice caves and sea ice around the coasts of Antarctica are rapidly melting. Large blocks of ice are breaking away from the ice mass. Coastal areas around the world are threatened by rising sea levels.

Krill

Antarctic krill live in huge, dense shoals in the waters of the Southern Ocean around Antarctica. They feed on microscopic plants and algae. Algae take in carbon dioxide and water and convert it into sugar, which they use to grow and reproduce. Algae also convert carbon dioxide into oxygen, which they release back into the atmosphere. The krill digest algae and excrete carbon. The carbon falls to the seabed, where it remains trapped for thousands of years. Krill therefore play an important role in taking carbon out of the atmosphere, which reduces global warming. Krill are the staple food of larger sea creatures, which are in turn eaten by bigger predators. Krill are one of the most successful and useful creatures on the planet. If they die out, the marine life that depends on them will also become extinct.

In recent years, some scientists have suggested that krill numbers have already decreased in the Antarctic. This is partly because their breeding and feeding grounds — the shallow waters around the icy coast of Antarctica — have been damaged by the rising temperatures of the Southern Ocean. Another reason is that fishing fleets harvest

THE IMPORTANCE OF KRILL

Estimated annual consumption of krill by different species, in million tons:

seals	69-143 tons (63-130 tonnes)
whales	37-47 tons (34-43 tonnes)
birds	16-22 tons (15-20 tonnes)
squid	0-110 tons (0-100 tonnes)
fish	0-22 tons (0-20 tonnes)

about 110,231 tons (100,000 tonnes) of krill each year. They are used for fish meal, which is used on fish farms, and for human consumption.

If we do nothing, the outlook for krill and the marine life that depends on it is bleak. However, some scientists believe that krill might actually offer a solution to the threat of global warming. Experiments have shown that if small quantities of iron are added to areas around Antarctica where krill live, the numbers of krill increase. The more krill there are, the more carbon is removed from the atmosphere and sent to the bottom of the ocean.

Krill are an important food source for animals in the Antarctic, including fish, penguins, seals, and baleen whales. Those animals cannot feed directly on microscopic algae, but the krill converts the energy contained within algae into a form that larger animals can use.

Threatened Antarctic Species

Antarctica is the southernmost continent on Earth. It is also the planet's highest, windiest, and driest continent. Its flora is very limited and includes some grasses, lichens, moss, and algae. Its animals include six species of penguin, seals, several species of whale, dolphins, and about 50 species of bird. Antarctica is home to 160 fish species, specially adapted to life at the low temperatures of the continent's coastal waters.

International agreements protect the flora and fauna of Antarctica. The International Union for Conservation and Nature lists some albatross species and giant southern petrels as endangered. Both birds are scavengers. They follow fishing fleets to snatch fish from their massive nets. Sometimes they become entangled in the long lines used by commercial fishing boats.

COMMERCIAL LONG-LINE FISHING

Because species such as the albatross are threatened by long-line fishing, countries that use this method have agreed on several policies to help prevent bird deaths. Long-line fishermen must:

- Frighten birds away with streamers attached behind their boats.
- Weigh their lines so that they sink faster and birds don't see them.
- Dump waste away from land, where fewer birds will be attracted to the lines.
- Put their lines out at night when there are fewer birds scavenging.

Emperor penguins are protected by international treaties but are nevertheless considered by some countries to be endangered. This is because of the danger to their habitat. Large areas of sea ice disappear each year. Another threat is the decline in the numbers of krill, a key part of their diet.

A king penguin gives a fur seal a piece of its mind. Rising sea temperatures are already affecting the delicate Antarctic ecosystem. In the future, these two species will have to compete ever more fiercely for food and territory.

The fur seal is also dependent on krill for part of its diet. By the beginning of the 20th century, the fur seal had been hunted to near extinction. Commercial seal hunting was banned in the early 1900s, and fur seal numbers have recovered rapidly since then. The seal's recovery may also be due, in part, to declining whale numbers in the Antarctic. Hunting reduced the whale population, making it easier for the fur seals to find food.

Governments around the world are now aware of the importance of keeping this last wilderness safe. The Antarctic Treaty System is a series of international agreements among 46 countries. It regulates fishing, protects flora and fauna, and controls the activities of visitors to Antarctica and what they may take there. Dumping waste in Antarctica and in the waters around it is prohibited.

The main threat to all the species that dwell in Antarctica comes from the rising sea temperatures around the landmass. As temperatures rise, the air around the Antarctic fills with moisture, and snow forms over the land. This alters the delicately balanced ecosystem of Antarctic plants and animals. Snow may damage penguin nests. Melting ice caves in the pack ice reduce the nursery grounds for young krill. Warmer waters allow new predators to move in and new plants to gain a foothold.

WARMING WATERS

As the sea around Antarctica warms, it will cause major changes to the local ecosystem. A rise of just 1.8° Fahrenheit (1° Celsius) will enable new predators, previously incapable of surviving the Antarctic winter, to move into the area. Sharks and king crabs will be able to live and hunt in the coastal waters, where they will disrupt food chains. The invaders will compete with seabirds, seals, and whales for the fish and shellfish that live there.

Bigger or Smaller?

Antarctica is a highly complex ecosystem. Some scientists disagree with the commonly held view that the ice cap is shrinking as the planet heats up. They claim that the ice cap is actually getting thicker. As the sea warms up, the usually very dry air becomes moist. The water vapor in the air turns to snow and snow layers add to the layers of ice inland. So although the ice sheets of Antarctica are receding toward the South Pole, they are growing higher. That might actually offset the threat of rising sea levels. In support of this more optimistic view, some studies suggest that numbers of fur seals and emperor penguins have actually increased.

Humans in Antarctica

So far, human contact with the Antarctic has not posed a threat to the wildlife there. Humans have never established settlements in Antarctica. Researchers are allowed to spend time on the continent, but it's rare for more than 400 people to live there at any one time. In 2007, about 37,000 tourists went to Antarctica for very brief visits, never staying overnight. Antarctica remains the last true wilderness on Earth.

An aircraft runway that opened in 2008 could change the situation. Although it was built to transport researchers and their equipment, it may only be a matter of time before more tourists arrive. In 2007, Japanese whaling ships entered the area with the intention of hunting whales, claiming it was for scientific purposes.

A passenger jet sits on the ice runway waiting to collect scientists from the Australian research center in Antarctica. The scientists have been studying the effects of climate change on the continent.

Like other wildernesses, Antarctica may have reserves of oil or other valuable minerals. Mining and oil companies may be tempted to exploit these in the decades to come. Commerce and tourism are likely to bring humans into increasing contact with the Antarctic in the future. Its plants and animals will likely pay the price.

WHAT WOULD YOU DO?

You Are in Charge

Your school is arranging a trip to the Antarctic. Before you decide to join them, you should consider the following:

- This isn't like a trip to an African wildlife reserve, for example, where local people and wildlife benefit from well-managed ecotourism. Antarctica has no locals who benefit.
- Every footstep on the Antarctic surface can cause damage. Every dumped piece of waste from passing ships will pollute the sea.
- We don't know how long Antarctica will remain as undamaged as it is now. This may be your only opportunity to visit.

In what ways could your visit to the Antarctic be beneficial? How can you be sure that you are causing as little damage as possible?

Glossary

algae Very simple plants that have no stems or leaves but that photosynthesize (use sunlight as a source of energy)

amphibians Animals that can live both in water and on land

aquatic Water based

bottom trawling A fishing method that involves towing trawl nets along the sea floor

carrion The rotting flesh of a dead animal

cash crops Crops that farmers grow to sell rather than for their own consumption

critically endangered Describing a species whose numbers have fallen so low that there is a strong chance that it will become extinct

cull Reduce the numbers of a species by killing some

ecological zones Areas where a particular kind of ecology exists, such as savannahs or coral reefs

ecologists Scientists who study ecosystems

ecosystems All the plants and animals in an area that depend upon one another and their environment for food and shelter

ecotourism A form of tourism that aims to minimize ecological damage to the natural environment

endangered At risk of being wiped out

exploit Use or develop something in order to gain a benefit

extinct Describing a species of plant or animal that once existed but that has died out

fauna All the animal life of a region

flora All the plant life of a region

food chain A hierarchy of living things, each of which feeds on the one below

Greenpeace An international organization that takes nonviolent direct action to protect the environment

habitat The natural conditions and environment of an animal or plant

humid The oppressive state of higher-than-normal moisture in the air

Ice Age One of several periods in Earth's history when temperatures fell worldwide and large areas of Earth's surface were covered with ice sheets

inbreeding The mating of closely related individuals of a species

indigenous Plants or animals that are native to a place

invasive species Non-native species of plants or animals that out-compete native species in a specific habitat

krill A tiny marine creature similar to a shrimp

logging Cutting down trees to sell the wood

long-line fishing A commercial fishing technique that uses hundreds or even thousands of baited hooks hanging from a single long line

marine Of the sea

open-cast mining Extracting metals or minerals from the ground by removing surface layers rather than by making tunnels underground

pollutants Any substances that when introduced to an environment damage the health of the organisms that live there

predators Animals that eat other animals

quotas Limitations that have been imposed on the quantity of something

savannah A grassy plain with few trees, in tropical and subtropical regions

scavengers Animals that eat the dead remains and wastes of other animals and plants

species A class of organism containing individuals that resemble one another and may interbreed

sustainable A way of life that exploits natural resources without destroying the ecological balance of a particular area

Further Information

Books

Butterfield, Moira. *Rainforests in Danger* (Franklin Watts, 2004)

Garbutt, Nick. *100 Animals to See Before they Die* (Bradt, 2007)

Sachidhanandam, Uma. *Green Alert! Threatened Habitats* (Raintree, 2004)

Wagner, Vigi. *Endangered Species: Opposing Viewpoints.* (Greenhaven, 2007)

Web Sites

Endangered Species
www.endangeredspecie.com
Search this resource for specific endangered species in your state. Learn more by using the site's list for further reading and links to related organizations.

Kids Planet
www.kidsplanet.org
Learn more about endangered animals by reviewing the facts on this site. Kids Planet includes suggestions for getting involved, debates the issues of animal adoption, and offers a list of resources.

National Wildlife Federation
www.nwf.org
Encourage the conservation of endangered species with the help of generous resources provided by this nonprofit organization.

Wildlife Conservation Society
ww.wcs.org
Help save wildlife in your state by learning more about local and national conservation efforts.

Save the Rainforest
www.savetherainforest.org
Learn more about rain forest ecosystems on this web site with information about the consequences of its loss.

Greenpeace
www.greenpeace.org
Get involved in efforts to improve conditions for at-risk wildlife. Take steps to reduce global warming and improve the environment.

Publisher's note to educators and parents: Our editors have carefully reviewed these web sites to ensure that they are suitable for children. Many web sites change frequently, however, and we cannot guarantee that a site's future contents will continue to meet our high standards of quality and educational value. Be advised that children should be closely supervised whenever they access the Internet.

What Would You Do?

Page 11:
You could look into other ways of making money from the forest. Ecotourism is one possibility. Other options include finding buyers for rain forest products, such as medicines or Brazil nuts. Growing crops in the shade of the outer forest is another way of making some cash for the community. Fair Trade organizations also sell textiles or other handicrafts made by local communities, investing as much profit as possible back into the village.

Page 17:
Many big engineering projects have been prevented when sufficient numbers of people oppose them. If people can show that a species of plant or animal will be critically endangered by engineering work, the work may be halted to allow a study to be done. An Internet or national press campaign can be very effective. Organizations such as the World Wildlife Fund can put pressure on countries whose funds are assisting the development. A famous movie star or some other international personality could also draw attention to your cause.

Page 23:
Environmental groups might support the request from Inuit groups to allow them to increase their catch. The Inuit hunt in small boats and catch only as much as they need or as their countries' quotas allow. Environmental groups would oppose plans by other whale-hunting countries. Other countries have alternative food sources and, while whale numbers may be increasing, we have no way of knowing if modern methods of whaling are sustainable. Whales are slow to reach adulthood and to begin breeding. Whale-watching businesses would point out the economic value of high whale populations. Students could suggest that Japan or Norway may better profit from whale-watching and ecotourism than by hunting whales for their meat or byproducts.

Page 33:
It would certainly help to ban people from certain areas of forest regularly used by migrating elephants. This would greatly reduce the risk to elephants and humans. Building deeper wells in villages where elephants dwell would eliminate competition between humans and elephants for water. Still, there are rogue elephants that attack humans for no reason. Local authorities should deal with such situations quickly to prevent villagers from taking matters into their own hands.

Page 39:
This is a difficult issue. Many people would argue that park visitors should be able to use the country's wildlife areas. Raising the entrance fees might mean that only the rich could afford to use the parks. Closing the parks altogether might turn many people against the idea of wildlife reserves. Some compromises might be:

- Build stable, fenced walking routes.
- Recruit more park rangers and impose bigger fines for littering.
- Ban pets from the park.
- Limit access to highly popular areas such as rivers.
- Strictly control fishing to preserve fish stocks and riverbanks.

Page 45:
There are several arguments in favor of going. If more people see the stunning landscapes of the Antarctic, then more people will want to protect it from the bigger threats of oil and mineral exploitation and permanent settlements. Tourism brings in income to countries in the South Atlantic, giving those countries nearest to Antarctica an incentive to protect the region. You could check which company is organizing your trip and make sure that they have a good reputation. You might organize your fellow travelers and inform them about how to do the least damage while they are there: Leave nothing behind; don't touch animals or plants; don't remove anything.

Index

Page numbers in **bold** refer to illustrations.

Africa 4, 12–17
algae 18, **21**, 22, 40, 42
 blooms 22–23, **23**
amphibians 4, 5, 7
Antarctica 40–45
Arctic 20, 34–35
Arctic National Wildlife Refuge 34–35
Asia 4, 24–33

baiji 31, **31**
birds 5, 7, 11, 25, 34, **34**, 38, **39**, 40, 42
bison 36, **36**
black rhinoceros 12, 16–17, **16**

California condor 38, **39**
captive breeding programmes 17, 24, 28, 36, 38
Central America 4, 8
China 24, 26, 27, 28, 29
climate 4, 7, 18
climate change 4, 5, 7, 31
conservation 12, 24, 27, 29, 30, 33, 35, 38
coral 18, 20–21, **21**

dams 8, 17, 31
desert 12, 16
dolphins 8, 19, 31, **31**, 42

ecosystems 6, 18, 32, 43, 44
ecotourism 13, **13**, 30, 33, 45
elephant, African 12, 13, 15, 28
elephant, Asian 26, 28, 33
extinction 5, 7, 8, 12, 14, 18–19, 24, 29, 31, 36, 40, 43

farming 4, 8, 10, 11, 14–15, 26, 32, 41
fashion industry 28
fish 8, 18, 19, 20, 22, 25, 31, 38, 40, 42, 44
fishing 18–19, **19**, 20, 40–41, 42, 43
 overfishing 18–19
 quotas 19
floods 4, 14, 17
food chains 18, 22, 38, 40, 44
forest 14, 15, 16, 17, 30, 31, 33, 34
fur seal 43, **43**, 44
fur trade 32, **32**

Ganges River dolphin 31
global warming 4, 7, 18, 20, 21, 40, 41, 43, 44
greater bamboo lemur 15

habitat loss 4, 7, 8, 12, 16, 17, 20–21, 24, 26, 28, 30, 31, 42
harlequin frog 4, **6**, 7
hunting 12, 14, 15, 16, 20, 21, 23, 28, 30, 31, 32, 33, 36, 43

inbreeding 28
India 26, 28, 33
insects 4, 5, 6, 7
International Union for Conservation of Nature (IUCN) 12, 14, 16, 18, 20, 27, 30, 35, 42

invasive species 38, 43, 44

krill 40–41, **41**, 42, 43

lion 12, 13, 37
logging 4, **5**, 8, 9, 11, 14, 15, 16, 24, 28

Madagascar 14, 15
marshland 13, 34, 38
medicine 9, 11, 16, 18, 27, 28, 31
mining 8, 11, 14, 17, 45

North America 34–39

oceans 7, 18–23
 acidification of 21
oil 18, 34–35, **35**, 45
orangutans 24, **25**, 27, 30

panda 26, **26**, 27
penguins 40, 42, 43, **43**, 44
pink river dolphin 8
plants 4, 5, 6, 8, 9, **9**, 11, 14, 17, 27, 32, 38, 39, 42, 43
poaching 16, 17
polar bears 20
pollution 4, 8, 17, 18, 21, 22, **22**, 31, 32, 34, 38, 43, 45
population growth 14, 18, 32
proboscis monkey 30, **30**
pygmy hippo 12, 16

rain forests 4–11, 13, 18, 24
 clearance 4, 5, **5**, 7, 8, **8**, 9, **9**
 dwellers 10, **10**
rays 18, 19
Red List, the 12, 14, 18, 20, 27, 30, 35
reptiles 5, 25
rhino horn 12, 14, 16, 17
ring-tailed lemur **15**
rivers 8, 14, 17, 30, 31

savannah 12, 15, 16
seabirds 18, 19, 44
seals 20, 35, 40, 42, 43, **43**, 44
settlements 26, 28, 32, 33, 34, 37, 44
sharks 18, 19, 22, 44
shellfish 18, 21, 38, 44
short-tailed albatrosses **34**, 35
skins 14, 28
slender loris 31
snow leopard 32
South America 4, 8, 38

tiger 6, 26, 27, 28–29, **29**
tourism 11, 12, 13, 17, 18, 20, 21, 44, 45
trees 5, 7, 8, 10, 11, 14
turtles 18, 19, 22, 35

United States 17, 20, 27, 34–37, 38

whales 18, 20, 22, 35, 40, 42, 43, 44
whaling 18, 20, 23, 43, 44
wildlife parks 12, 17, 28, 36, 39
wildlife reserves 13, 14, 17, 24, 27, 28, 29, 30, 33, 35, 36, 38
wolves 37, **37**

zebra 12, 15
zoos 17, 27, 28, 29, 37, 38

About the Author
Sean Sheehan was a teacher in London and Southeast Asia before becoming a full-time writer, now based in Ireland. He has written numerous books for young readers, specializing in geography and history.